The Unstuck Process

ROBERT MIDDLETON

The

Unstuck Process

*12 Powerful Questions That
Create Breakthrough Results*

Copyright Notice

Copyright © 2014 Robert Middleton. All rights reserved.

Published by The Unstuck Process
210 Riverside Drive
Boulder Creek, CA 95006
www.theunstuckprocess.com

Layout and design by Robert Middleton
Cover Design by Thomas McGeee

This book, or parts thereof may not be reproduced in any form without permission from the publisher. Exceptions are made for brief excerpts used in published reviews.

This book is available at quantity discounts for bulk purchases. For information, email: apm@actionplan.com

Warning!

This book outlines a process designed to alter your perceptions of limiting beliefs that are preventing you from living a fuller life and experiencing greater success. No claims to its efficacy can be guaranteed, as we cannot control how you implement the process. However, we can guarantee that if you do not apply the process as outlined in the book, that you have no right to expect any results whatsoever.

All the best,

Robert Middleton

ISBN-13: 978-1502572684
ISBN-10: 1502572680

To Byron Katie, Rupert Spira and Arjuna Ardagh
Without them, this book would have been impossible.

Contents

Contents	1
Before You Read this Book	3
Introduction to the Unstuck Process	5
1. Where Are You Stuck?	11
2. What Are You Feeling?	17
3. How Do You Behave?	21
4. What Is the Belief?	25
5. Is the Belief True?	33
6. Is this Belief Working for You?	37
7. What Are the Costs?	41
8. What is the Payoff?	45
9. Who Would You Be Without this Belief?	53
10. What Possibilities Might Open Up to You?	57
11. Is it Just OK to Be Who You Are?	59
12. What Will You Do Next?	61
About You	63
Take Action	64
Acknowledgements	65
All the Questions & Sub-Questions	66
About Robert Middleton	71

This had better be good!

Before you read this book...

The sad truth is that most self-help books don't help you much. It's not that they don't say helpful things, provide useful insights, or offer specific things you can do to make positive changes in your life.

However, most self-help books say too much, give too many ideas and offer more things to implement than the average person will ever apply in their lifetimes. And as a result, we get overwhelmed and implement very little from these books.

I decided to make this book different. This book outlines one simple but powerful step-by-step process to help get past stuckness and avoidance behavior. The process consists of 12 questions that you answer one at a time. And then I take a few pages to explain each question in enough detail so that virtually any intelligent person can answer the questions.

Do not read this book for entertainment. It's a very simple guide. And it will only work for you if you actually answer all of the questions about where you're stuck and what you're avoiding in your life. If it "takes" you might do what I and others have done and ask and answer these questions frequently, anytime you get stuck or find yourself avoiding things.

If you do, you just may discover a world without stuckness or avoidance. **And that is a wonderful world, indeed.**

Have fun with the process!

Robert Middleton

Introduction to *The Unstuck Process*

One weekday afternoon sometime in 2003, I sat in my home office, as stuck as I'd ever been. All productive work had ground to a halt several days before, and I was feeling down, frustrated, overwhelmed, stuck. I could barely get through the routine tasks of the day, such as checking email. And instead of working, I avoided almost everything.

A number of important tasks and projects that had seen no progress for over a week languished on my to-do list. And every time I looked at the list, I felt more hopeless than the moment before.

Then I remembered something.

During the past year I had been working with a process designed to get one past limiting and stressful beliefs. I had used it a number of times with some success, even with clients, but this time was different: I was as intractably stuck as I'd ever been. So I decided to give the process a try.

I pulled out the worksheet to go through the steps of this written process. It included several questions that I answered by writing them down.

It took me some time to find the answer to the fourth question that was the foundation of the process. But it finally clicked and I moved forward. In about half an hour I had answered the remaining questions.

Once I was done, I sat there wordless for several minutes. In that short span, something had shifted. The doom and gloom that had hung over me for the past few weeks lifted like the fog on a sunny day.

I looked out at the world through different eyes, with different thoughts, with different feelings.

And then I turned my attention to my to-do list. My hopeless feelings were replaced by hopeful ones. Items that had seemed impossible to accomplish seemed ridiculously easy. And by the end of the day, I had completed everything I had been putting off for so long.

If I'd only gotten that one result from doing this process I'd, have been more than satisfied. But that was only the beginning.

For the next several months, I experienced an explosion of productivity and creativity unlike anything I'd experienced before. My business took off as I created new programs and services, and my income increased and then doubled over two years. I initiated several large projects and succeeded at all of them with very little struggle. Everything flowed.

These results got my attention, to put it mildly. And whenever I felt down or stuck and started to avoid things, I'd simply apply the process again with similar results.

Over the past several years I've also done a lot of tinkering with the process. I wanted to make it easier and even more effective. I tested it on my clients with similar results. I wrote about it in my newsletter and blog. I led workshops and created programs that integrated this process.

Ultimately I called it the Unstuck Process.

And that brings me to today. It seemed the most logical next step would be to write a little book about this process and explain, in simple step-by-step language, how it works and how you can integrate it into your life.

The process that I used that day was "The Work" of Byron Katie that I learned in 2002. As I said, it consisted of a few simple but powerful questions that can result in a dramatic and often life-changing shift in perspective. Her ground-breaking book, *Loving What Is,* is the definitive guide to her work.

Over the years I adapted the process for my clients and me, but the essence is the same; it's about inquiry, about exploring the thoughts and beliefs that drive our feelings and behavior.

The main difference is that I applied The Work to the domain of productivity and success; Katie's primary focus has always been on relationships and the stressful beliefs that undermine them.

As a business and marketing consultant and coach, I found that a large number of my clients struggled with implementing what they had learned from me.

What good does it do to have a new marketing message and marketing plan, if you don't implement it? For years I was puzzled that people with equal intelligence and potential could get such different results. One client would apply some knowledge and realize great success. Another would learn the same things and get nowhere.

When I discovered Byron Katie's Work, it unlocked the key.

The only significant difference between two people is not their education or background or life circumstances, but their beliefs, or more accurately the degree of attachment to their beliefs. And beliefs, feelings and actions are strongly correlated, as we'll explore in this book.

For instance, if you believe you are not "the marketing type," you will tend to lack confidence about your marketing efforts and you'll also tend to avoid doing certain marketing activities. As a result, you won't get the marketing results you want.

Of course, this applies to every field of human endeavor, both professional and personal. Your beliefs shape your results, not sometimes, but every time.

I titled this book The Unstuck Process because being stuck is exactly how you feel when you hold onto a limiting or constrictive belief. I often amaze my clients by how easily I can identify their state of mind and their beliefs by where they're stuck in their marketing!

Once someone learns how to dissolve limiting beliefs,

avoidance disappears as well. What remains are unlimited possibilities for accomplishment, well being and fulfillment.

Despite the power of this process, this is not a panacea or cure-all for human ills. It is definitely not a new belief system. It is simply a powerful practice that anyone can use.

The format of this book is very simple: it's based on each of the twelve questions in the Unstuck Process. The better you understand each of these questions, the easier it will be to answer them and the better results you'll get.

Here are the 12 questions:

    1. Where are you stuck, or what are you avoiding?

    2. What is your primary feeling when you experience this?

    3. How do you behave when you experience this?

    4. What is the belief underneath the avoidance?

    5. You're convinced the belief is true, but is it?

    6. Is this belief working for you?

    7. What are the costs of attaching to this belief?

    8. a) What is the payoff of attaching to this belief?
       b) Is the payoff real and is it worth it?

    9. Who would you be and how would things be, if it were impossible to attach to this belief?

    10. What possibilities might open up to you, if you no longer identified with this belief?

    11. It is OK just to be who you are without having this belief anymore?

    12. What will you do next?

As we explore these questions and learn the process, I invite you to join me in a world without stuckness.

You may want to download the Unstuck Process Worksheet now to use as you go through the process:

www.actionplan.com/up/Unstuck_Process.doc

*Stuck in a box
with no way out.*

*Just when you thought you'd
never get stuck again.*

Question 1:
Where Are You Stuck?

The first question in the Unstuck Process is, "Where are you stuck, or what are you avoiding?"

We think of being stuck when writing something (writer's block), making an important decision, or moving forward with a big project. We're not getting any ideas and feel no inspiration. We feel stuck! We've all been there a thousand times.

Stuckness often feels like a physical force, holding us back, not being able to move forward. When we feel stuck we often feel overwhelmed, confused, frustrated and hopeless.

And when we feel stuck, the observable symptom is avoidance. We are avoiding that writing, making that decision or moving forward with the big project. Because taking these actions feels overwhelming or challenging, we avoid getting down to work. And, of course, the more we avoid, the more we feel stuck.

To better understand stuckness, it's useful to observe what we are avoiding. I use the word "avoidance" throughout the book and define it as: "deliberately avoiding, preventing from happening." Avoidance behavior is what you are not doing instead of taking action. And stuckness is the feeling that precedes avoidance. You may have thought of avoidance as occasional procrastination, something that you did when facing an unpleasant task. We avoid doing our taxes, taking out the garbage and going to the gym.

We see avoidance as an activity, not a symptom. And we easily justify avoidance. It's no big deal, we think; we'll get around to that task later. It won't have much of an impact on our lives, right?

So let's look at some areas where we avoid, many of which we don't even realize we are avoiding.

We avoid starting or initiating things

As small children we were creative bundles of energy and creativity. But as we get older, we play it safer and risk less. An idea of a project may flit through our consciousness only to be quashed a few moments later. Or we harbor a desire to do something big for many years but it never gets out of the dream phase. Every idea is a possibility, but of course it would be impossible and impractical to do everything; yet good ideas are suppressed almost every day of our lives.

We avoid completing things

Think of the number projects you started, from home improvements to learning a new language that you initiated but never completed. I can't tell you how many clients of mine were enthusiastic to start a new marketing campaign only to see it wither a month or two later. And every failure to complete a project saps our energy and enthusiasm.

We avoid important communication

It's almost a cliché to remember to tell our loved ones that we love them. But we put it off all the time. We intend to care more, spend more time with our children, thank someone or show gratitude to a friend. But it seems easier to avoid these things than to just do them.

We avoid the important stuff and do the trivial

The hallmark of avoidance behavior is engaging in low-value activities that give little real satisfaction. I've known very successful business people who fritter hours away on the Internet when a major proposal or project is due. Or instead of following up with a lead, they find the time to organize their files! This kind of avoidance feels addictive and compulsive, pushing us away from high-value activities.

We rarely fulfill New Year's resolutions

Most people give up on New Year's resolutions after a certain age because they never stick to them. The optimistic resolutions to lose weight, stop smoking and exercise more fall by the wayside almost immediately, soon followed by pessimistic attitudes where we give up before we even start.

Self-Improvement that goes nowhere

If you're reading this book, the odds are good that you've read more than one self-help book in your life. The truth is, we want to do better, accomplish more, make a difference and have our lives matter. But we abandon most of our self-improvement projects well before we see any positive results.

So where are you stuck?

Before we can get beyond stuckness we simply have to tell the truth about what we are avoiding. We need to state it and write it down. We don't have to embellish it or tell a story about it or justify it. And we can start anywhere. Much of our stuckness shows up in avoidance behavior. Start with simple things, like the following:

> I'm avoiding getting my closet organized
>
> I'm avoiding cleaning up the yard
>
> I'm avoiding looking at my son's homework
>
> I'm avoiding writing an article for my business
>
> I'm avoiding planning our next vacation
>
> I'm avoiding starting an investment plan
>
> I'm avoiding exercising every morning
>
> I'm avoiding going to the dentist
>
> I'm avoiding reading that business book
>
> I'm avoiding asking for a raise

If you take just a few minutes to reflect on stuckness and

avoidance, you might start to realize that you are avoiding a whole lot more than you realize. But with this process you just start with *one thing* you're avoiding.

What I discovered when I had my "stuckness breakthrough," is that by getting past the avoidance of doing the items on my to-do list, many other areas that were stuck effortlessly dropped away soon after. I can't promise that will happen to you, but for now, trust that this process will help you.

What I do recommend is that you pick something that's been bugging you for a while. It should be something you seem to have a fair amount of resistance to and that you've been struggling with.

Now pick the thing you've been avoiding and write it down on a piece of paper. You can also write it down on the Unstuck Process Worksheet that you can download here:

www.actionplan.com/up/Unstuck_Process.doc

Sub-Questions

This is not a rigid process, but a very flexible one. I've discovered that for most of the questions, you can ask "sub-questions" or even substitute a question to fit your particular situation. I recommend you start with the 12 "Core Questions" but then try other ones as you keep working with the process. Here are some alternate questions for question #1.

What more personal things are you avoiding?

The list above is mostly about external things you are avoiding, such as projects. But there are other, more subtle areas of avoidance. You may be avoiding intimacy in your relationship, or facing a conflict or difficult conversation. You might be avoiding getting into shape or eating better. Perhaps you're avoiding your spiritual practice or learning a new language. No matter what you are avoiding, in any area of your life, you can use the Unstuck Process.

What is something you are resisting?

Resistance is similar to avoidance. You might be actually doing something and not avoiding it, but resisting it, complaining about it, struggling with it. For instance, you might have something you do regularly in your job that you hate, so you suffer while doing it. So perform the process on that.

What is something you are doing that you don't want to be doing?

The things that come immediately to mind are various addictive habits that you do compulsively but wish you could stop. You might watch TV too much or spend a lot of time on the Internet, social media or YouTube. You'd rather be doing other things, but your time is occupied by these low-value activities. This could also include indulging in addictive substances, such as drugs and alcohol. (If this is the case, I recommend getting outside professional help with substance abuse.)

What is an attitude you have that's not working for you?

An attitude is defined as "a settled way of thinking or feeling about someone or something." Attitudes are similar to beliefs, but you'll usually find a belief under most attitudes. Common attitudes include: indifference, negativity, judgment, arrogance, pessimism, distractedness, conceitedness, being guarded, rudeness, reluctance, complacency, self-centeredness, etc. If you notice that you have a habitual attitude about something, start questioning that.

What are your judgments about other people?

This can be a vast area to explore. This is the area that Byron Katie mostly focuses on. Here are some of the questions she asks on her "Judge Your Neighbor Worksheet."

http://tinyurl.com/judge-neighbor

> Who angers, confuses or disappoints you and why?
>
> How do you want them to change? What do you want them

to do?

What advice would you offer them?

In order for you to be happy in this situation, what do you need them to think, say, feel, or do?

What do you think of them? (Don't be nice!)

Just answer one or more of these questions and then continue with the Unstuck Process.

The second core question, which I address in the next chapter, is about the feelings that are associated with stuckness and avoidance.

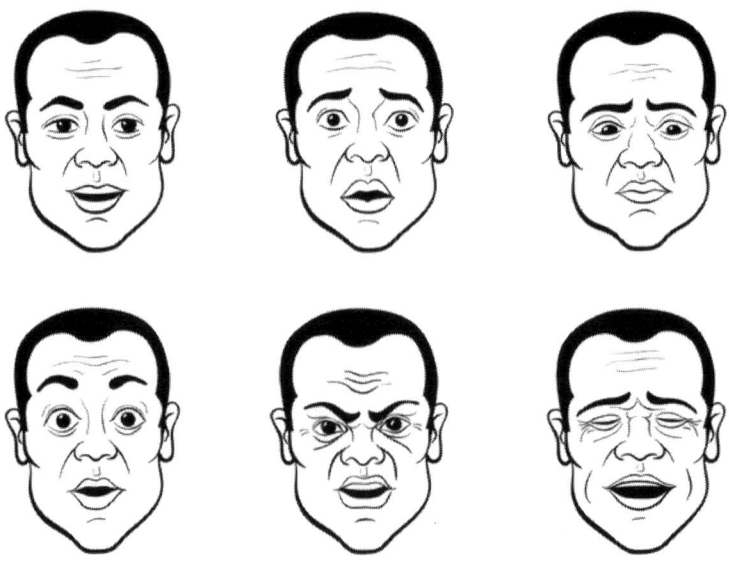

What are you feeling?

Question 2: *What Are You Feeling?*

The second question in the Unstuck Process is, "What is your primary feeling when you experience being stuck or avoiding?"

It would be unusual to avoid something and feel nothing. In fact, we often notice how we're feeling before we realize that the feeling is related to any kind of avoidance.

We may be feeling uneasy or frustrated or overwhelmed or confused or guilty or pressured or any number of feelings.

Of course, one of the most familiar feelings is stuckness itself. I define stuckness as "the constrictive feelings of being unable to move forward, feeling held back."

When I'm working with clients on this second question and I ask them how they feel, I often get a story instead:

> *"Well, there's so much to do right now, you have no idea, so when I think of doing that project it just seems impossible to me and I find a way of putting it off."*

"OK," I respond, "but how do you actually feel when you avoid doing that project? I'm looking for a feeling, not a story, what are you actually feeling inside?"

> *"Uh, I feel incredibly stuck! I feel held back, unable to move forward. I feel frustrated and thwarted."*

That's more like it. Those are real feelings you can experience.

But why is it important to identify the feeling associated with the avoidance? Because you want to make it real. Just naming and talking about the avoidance is often disconnected to your actual experience. All of those avoidances listed in the first chapter are attached to certain feelings or emotions. And those feelings are usually about something that happened in the past.

Let's look at one of them:

Avoiding getting the closet organized.

When you think about that avoidance, the feeling that may arise is defiance. Well, what's that about? As you think about organizing your closet and the feeling of defiance arises, you may recall your mother always telling you how to organize your closet when you were a teenager. You remember yelling at her, telling her you wanted to organize your closet your way.

Now all of this is much more real to you. It's starting to make sense why you are avoiding organizing your closet!

As insightful as this is, it's not necessary to connect your avoidance and feeling to an event in the past. Perhaps one will pop up for you, and that's fine. But if one doesn't pop up, that's fine as well. This process is not therapy designed to work out all the traumas of your childhood.

The Unstuck Process is about *experience.* It's about becoming fully aware of the complete experience in the present moment related to your avoidance.

In this process we face "what is." It's not about speculating about the past or future or trying to change anything or fix anything. It's not about any kind of manipulation, and it's really not even about self-improvement as we usually think of it.

Self-improvement is about adding something to yourself. Learning Spanish, or how to play the guitar, or getting better at relating to your wife is about self-improvement.

Nothing wrong with self-improvement; I heartily encourage it. But this process is about self-awareness. It's about clearly seeing what's in the way of being and expressing our true nature, which is naturally creative, capable and expansive.

Experience the Feeling

When we identify the feeling or feelings associated with the avoidance behavior, we are a little closer to experiencing what's veiling our true nature.

So take a look and "name that feeling." And then write it down on a sheet of paper or the worksheet.

And then take a few moments to let yourself really feel that feeling. Get out of your head and *feel* what happens when you're avoiding that thing. And let whatever associated thoughts or past experiences or judgments come up as well. Take whatever you get. Nothing that you experience is wrong.

If you work with a facilitator on this process they might encourage you to go deeper and share anything that comes up around the feelings, but the beauty of this process is that you can do it yourself and you don't really need to do more than feel the feeling as fully as you can.

Delving too deeply into past experiences is tricky. It can lead to blame or guilt and it can get you away from just experiencing.

Remember, a feeling is simple, like frustration, guilt, anger or stuckness. A feeling is not a story. Yes, you attach stories to feelings, but feelings stand on their own.

Sometimes you can start the Unstuck Process by identifying a feeling first. You may not be clear about the avoidance, but you know you don't feel good about something. You feel uneasy or frustrated or confused.

So start with the feeling and then ask yourself if the feeling is associated with any avoidance. For instance, if the feeling is "uneasy" then look to see what you're uneasy about. Perhaps it's that you didn't get back to someone you promised you'd follow-up with.

Sub-Questions

Some people find it difficult to articulate a feeling. Instead, they'll report on what they are thinking. If you can't find a feeling, try to locate a body sensation instead. And even if you *can* find a feeling, you might want to identify a body sensation as well to your observations for question #2.

What's the sensation in your body?

It might be heavy, or aching, or painful. Also, ask where it is in your body, what the intensity is and how big it is. For instance: "The sensation I feel in my body is a dull aching in my solar plexus, about the size of a baseball." Become more aware of that physical sensation and sense it in the same way you feel the feeling.

If you find it hard to come up with an answer to the first question about what you are avoiding, (or the alternates) you can start with the feeling or the sensation. "What are you feeling right now?" or "What are you sensing in your body right now?" And then you can come back to identifying the avoidance after that.

Now continue on to the next question in the process.

Once you've written down the feeling and experienced it as fully as you can, it's time to look at the reactions and behaviors that follow the feeling.

Question 3: How Do You Behave?

The third question in the Unstuck Process is, "How do you behave when you're avoiding?"

The obvious answer to this question is that you avoid doing something, the avoidance we identified with the first question.

But when you avoid, you don't just sit there! In turning away from something, we turn towards other things. We often turn to busywork, the Internet or cleaning.

Yes, cleaning! One of my sayings is, "If you have a completely neat desk, you're probably avoiding your marketing!"

The Avoidance Scenario

Included in avoidance behavior is thinking associated thoughts and feeling related feelings. Let's take the example of avoiding organizing your closet.

> **Avoidance:** Organizing the closet.
>
> **Feeling:** Defiance
>
> **Body:** Tense
>
> **Avoidance behavior:** Getting impatient with husband, eating a candy bar, watching TV, browsing Facebook
>
> **Related thoughts and feelings:** Resentment and blame towards others.

Now, like all the other parts of this "avoidance scenario," everything is happening very automatically. We don't think anything like the following:

> "Wow, my closet is a mess which makes me feel really defiant because it reminds me when my Mom told me how to clean my closet. I don't want to face this right now, so I'll go bitch at my husband, eat some candy and watch TV as I browse Facebook! And then, as a finishing touch, I'll add some resentment and blame directed towards my kids who have messy closets."

No, the feelings and reactions just happen. We don't even realize that these things are related to each other. But by stepping back with this process we start to put the pieces together. We "unbundle the experience" by deliberately slowing things down and taking a closer look at what's going on.

Remember, we don't need to come to any conclusions here or make any decisions about what we should do. Just do the process, one simple question at a time and answer as honestly as you can.

What does your avoidance scenario look like? You have three of the major pieces of the puzzle now. Before you just noticed some type of avoidance. But now you also see the associated feelings, reactions and behaviors associated with that avoidance.

At this point you may start to feel a little bit of freedom in relation to this avoidance scenario. You may be able to see how ludicrous it really is.

But then again, maybe not. Relax; we're not done yet. We have nine more questions in the process that explore the consequences of this scenario and the possibilities beyond the scenario.

Before you move to the next question, write out your whole avoidance scenario, with a detailed description of how you behave, including additional thoughts and feelings.

Write it on a piece of paper or on the worksheet.

Sub-Questions

You have a lot of leeway here. You're trying to get a clear picture of what actually happens when you are avoiding or resisting, doing something you don't want to be doing, or being stuck in an attitude.

What you don't want to do here is explain or analyze:

"Oh, I'm finding all kinds of other things to do instead; that's what I want to try to stop; my mother always did this as well; maybe this is hereditary."

None of that helps you. You just want to list the facts as if an outside observer were reporting on exactly what they saw. Imagine a closed circuit camera was watching you. What would it see?

You might ask any of these sub-questions to get clarity here:

> Describe your avoidance behavior in detail.
>
> What else are you avoiding when you avoid that?
>
> Is there an attitude or mindset associated with the avoidance?
>
> Is this behavior habitual and automatic?
>
> What are you thinking or saying to yourself when you're avoiding?
>
> Does your mood change when you're avoiding?

Be like a detective who is closely observing the evidence. But don't make any conclusions yet.

The next question, number four, may be the most important question in this process. It's about the beliefs that drive the avoidance in the first place.

*His belief loomed over him
like a menacing presence.*

Question 4: *What Is the Belief?*

The fourth question in the Unstuck Process is, "What is the belief underneath the avoidance?"

Now that we've identified the avoidance and the feeling associated with it, we want to find the belief that is driving the avoidance.

At the heart of this process are the beliefs that underlie your avoidance and feelings. Whenever we point to an action or avoidance, we will find a belief.

When a door is more than a door

You might put beliefs into three categories:

> **Neutral Beliefs** – That is a door; she is a woman; I have a headache.
>
> **Expansive Beliefs** – I can do it; this sandwich is incredible; he's an amazing person.
>
> **Constrictive Beliefs** – I'm hopeless at math; nobody understands me; she's a heartless bitch.

Here are some examples of neutral, expansive and constrictive beliefs all around the same thing, a door. A door is just a door, but with different kinds of beliefs, we see the door differently.

For instance, the word "door" is simply a word to represent the actuality of a certain kind of shape and energy. It's a word-symbol for something that we perceive. And it's useful to have names for things and people and concepts in order to navigate life and communicate in the everyday world.

Expansive beliefs add a positive attribute to something. Now it's "an awesome door, a beautiful door, a wonderful door." This point of view simply attaches a positive emotion to a person, thing or concept. Nothing wrong with that. With expansive beliefs we may experience things as pleasant and delightful.

Constrictive beliefs add a negative attribute to something. Now it's "a bad door, an ugly door or a useless door." This can be useful in its place as well. However with constrictive beliefs we will usually see things in a limited way. The classic such belief is, "Life it hard and then you die." Some people actually have this as their fundamental philosophy!

We get into trouble, as a general rule, when we attach negative attributes to others and ourselves. "I'm a loser, I can't make this work, and I'll be rejected," are constrictive beliefs that lead to avoidance and feelings of fear, anger and other negative emotions. A belief of this kind closes down possibilities outside of its own point of view.

Henry Ford once said, "If you say you can or you say you can't, you're right." I once had that saying on a small sign hanging on my wall. When you say you can't, that's clearly a limiting belief. When you say you can, it's an expansive belief. And you can expect your results to conform with whichever belief you identify with the most.

I've observed, with hundreds of clients, that they invariably hold a limiting belief of some kind that precedes the avoidance and their feeling about it.

In fact, it usually follows this pattern, like clockwork:

    1. Something triggers a limiting belief

    2. I'm convinced this belief is true

    3. I feel a constrictive feeling related to that belief

    4. I avoid taking action or moving forward

Let's look at an example of a belief from our list in chapter one.

I'm avoiding planning our next vacation.

What would you have to believe to avoid planning your vacation? It could be a number of things.

> I don't like vacations
>
> Vacations are a hassle
>
> Our vacations are never fun
>
> Vacations cost too much
>
> We never go where I want to go

Each of those statements could clearly trigger the avoidance of planning your vacation, couldn't they?

But, you protest, all of those are true! Well, are they? How do we determine if a belief is true or not?

One rule of thumb is that if the belief triggers a negative or stressful feeling, then it's not true. The belief is a reaction, not a statement of fact. After all, you could list a number of statements of fact about your vacations:

> When we go on vacations, we usually go camping
>
> Our vacations cost, on average, $2,000.
>
> Vacations take me about 5 hours to plan.
>
> I want to go to France for a vacation, you don't.

Those aren't beliefs; they are simply facts, right?

Now, we could also have expansive beliefs about vacations:

> I love vacations, because I get a break from work
>
> Vacations are an adventure
>
> Our vacations are always fun
>
> Vacations are affordable
>
> We always go where I want to go

These are not necessarily statements of fact, but they tend to lead to more positive experiences.

Also note that a couple might go on vacation together and see the same sights and eat the same food yet have completely opposite experiences. They both went on the same vacation but their experience was shaped by their beliefs. One person had a great time and the other was miserable.

When we identify the belief we are holding about a particular avoidance, we gain some deeper insight into our behavior.

The belief I identified when I did this process many years ago was along these lines; "I'm just not able to handle it all." And I felt overwhelmed. I felt completely stuck and had a hard time doing anything.

To progress successfully with this process, it's important that you identify the belief that is driving your avoidance. If you come up with the wrong belief, the whole process may miss the mark. When I did this process years ago, I tried several beliefs before I hit on the right one.

So what's the right belief?

It's the one you are actually believing. You don't need to figure it out; you need to observe it. But sometimes it's a little tricky to hit the nail on the head. The reason is that although the belief is in operation, it's sometimes not conscious; it's operating slyly in the background.

I ask clients to tell me what they tend to say to themselves when they are avoiding something. I get them talking and before too long, it just pops out.

Core beliefs underneath avoidance

I've found that the following three core beliefs are both common and pervasive:

- Fear of Communication/Connection
- Fear of Creativity/Self-Expression
- Fear of Action/Success

They then generate a wide variety of limiting beliefs that result in feelings of stuckness and avoidance behavior. The following are very common among people who are avoiding marketing their services:

Fear of Communication/Connection

> I'll be rejected or ridiculed
> Others won't accept me
> Others don't appreciate me
> Others don't understand me

Fear of Creativity/Self-Expression

> I'm not good at this
> I don't know enough
> I'm not creative enough
> It's not perfect yet

Fear of Action/Success

> I don't know how to do it
> I'll make a mistake
> It's too hard; I'll fail at it
> If I succeed, then what?

These beliefs will often be oriented to a perceived unpleasant outcome if you take action.

Below are some beliefs my clients have told me based on the three core fears outlined above:

Fear of Communication/Connection: Talking to someone might result in humiliation; making follow-up calls will end up in rejection; giving a presentation may lead to embarrassment.

Fear of Creativity/Self-Expression: Writing an article might subject me to judgment by my peers; the topics I write about aren't interesting; Nobody will like my website.

Fear of Action/Success: Promotion of any kind will make people think I'm desperate; working hard on my marketing won't amount to anything, anyway; If I succeed, then success and money will taint me.

These beliefs are simply expressions of what people think will happen if they took action instead of avoiding.

What is very clear is that these beliefs and others stop my clients dead in their tracks. When they believe these beliefs they will act consistently with them – that is, they will avoid taking action that might lead to unpleasant experiences.

And remember, these beliefs are held by people who really want to succeed, want to attract new clients and make a difference. These are not inherently lazy or delusional people. Often they built their businesses by word-of-mouth but are deathly afraid of putting themselves out there.

Now, take a few minutes to articulate a belief that is driving your avoidance. Write it down on a paper or the worksheet.

Do your best, but don't worry if it's perfect. With a few tries it will usually emerge.

Sub-Questions

This question about beliefs may be the most important in the process. The first three questions are like "bread crumbs" that lead us to the belief that is driving our behavior and avoidance. Until we see beneath the behavior and notice the belief, it is running the show.

People can more easily observe their avoidance behavior, their feelings related to this behavior, and their other actions related to avoidance, but most often have no clue as to what's triggering that behavior.

I often get comments, like: "I had no idea I believed that. In fact, I thought I believed the opposite."

In trying to identify the belief, we might struggle with the right wording or come up with a number of beliefs. But this is not a matter of guesswork; it's a matter of clear observation.

So you might ask a few questions to help you get to the belief:

What am I telling myself when I'm avoiding that thing; what is a phrase I keep repeating inside my head?

If we notice closely, we are always having running conversations inside our heads. And much of that conversation is a litany of limiting beliefs. Start noticing your thoughts more closely. What are you telling yourself most of the time, especially when you are avoiding?

Can I find the belief underneath my feeling?

A feeling of confusion might translate to, "I'll never understand this." A feeling of anger might translate into, "Doing this is beneath me." A feeling of antipathy might translate into, "This is a total waste of time." And an ongoing feeling of resistance may translate to, "This just isn't worth doing."

What would I have to believe to continue avoiding that activity?

Forgetting to do that project might translate to: "This project isn't important." Always saying I don't have time to get it done may be a smokescreen for something that feels very intimidating to do, and the belief might be, "I'll fail at it anyway, so what's the use?"

It's important that you really nail down this belief before continuing with the process, as it's the central hub around which everything else revolves.

In the fifth chapter we'll start questioning the validity of your belief.

*Don't believe everything you think;
you may be very wrong.*

Question 5: Is the Belief True?

The fifth question in the Unstuck Process is, "You're convinced the belief is true, but is it?"

If you're not really convinced that the belief is true (at least for now), perhaps you haven't quite zeroed in on the belief yet. A limiting belief has a kind of "sting" to it. It's stressful to believe that belief.

A belief is something you could argue for. A belief is something you would "bet your car" on. A belief is something you might even sacrifice your life for, yes, even if it's a negative, fearful and limiting belief. Sounds crazy, but read on.

I'm not exaggerating in any way here. Strong beliefs and convictions lead to extreme actions and avoidance.

If you truly believe, "It won't work anyway," you are taking a strong stand for unworkability. You are not reporting objectively on the way things are. You are shaping the way things are through your belief. You are causing yourself to become stuck.

Remember, some situation or thought triggers the belief, and in an instant you feel the feelings corresponding with the belief. Not long after, you are doing and saying things totally consistent with the belief, which is often avoidance behavior.

For instance, you remember that you haven't done your taxes and the deadline is looming, and the belief, "Doing taxes is a complete waste of time," just pops into your head automatically. And then you complain to your spouse: "I have to do my damn taxes, what a complete waste of time." And then instead of digging out your tax documents, you find yourself surfing social media for the next two hours.

As far as you're concerned, this belief doesn't *feel* true. It *is* true! And you can make a very strong argument for this belief. So even though surfing social media is also a time-waster, it's easy to do and doesn't trigger any resistance.

And what if someone contradicts your belief?

"Don't be so such a complainer," says your wife, "doing your taxes doesn't take that much time!"

And you reply, "You just don't understand. Every time I do my taxes, it takes hours. And I'm not very good at it anyway, and I always make some mistake or other. No, it's a waste of time, trust me!"

And from that point of view it's unlikely you'll ever just do your taxes without all that angst. That wouldn't make sense as it contradicts your belief. And to contradict a belief is to contradict your very self.

To be taken or caught up with a belief like this is a state called "identification." You no longer *have* a belief; you *are* the belief. And as far as you're concerned, no possibility outside of this belief is worth considering.

"I believe what I believe completely, totally, and absolutely."

It's not a lot of fun trying to communicate with a person with a belief this firm, this intractable. And it can be frustrating because you see how this belief is limiting someone, cutting off alternate possibilities and shutting the door to making anything creative or constructive happen.

Another way of looking at a belief is imagining it to be like fog. Fog obscures our view so we can't see what's behind the fog. Behind the fog lies reality but until the fog lifts we can't see that reality.

A belief is also like a stone in your shoe. You're walking along and a little stone gets into your shoe and suddenly you can't walk so well. But you don't realize it's a stone, it's hurting and affecting your walking without you knowing what it is. After awhile you just get used to it, even though it's still hampering your ability to walk.

The hypnosis of belief

Perhaps, most accurately, a belief is like a hypnotic trance. Everyone else can see that you're in a trance, but you can't. You say and do things that conform to the belief, but these things don't make the most sense or get the best results.

In working with one of my clients, this belief emerged: "It's not worth it, what's the use, it's a waste of time."

This was triggered by the thought of giving live talks and presentations. As soon as he thought of putting together a presentation, he felt the heebie jeebies. And then, without thinking about it, he started to work on something else instead.

As someone who has had tremendous success with using presentations to market my professional services, I knew that it wasn't a waste of time, but a very productive use of time.

But beliefs are not necessarily logical. When you're caught in the hypnotic spell of a belief, it's easy to argue against doing something, even if it's beneficial. Reason doesn't even come into the picture.

When I asked my client this question, "You're convinced this belief is true, but is it?" it momentarily broke the hypnotic trance. I wasn't telling him that his belief was wrong or giving him an alternative belief, just asking him if it was true or not, no matter how much he was convinced it was true.

He had to admit that he couldn't be sure that it was true.

After this exchange, I made the following comments:

"No, your belief seems true, but so does a dream at night until you wake up and realize it's a dream. You've been telling yourself that this was true for a long time; you have a lot invested in this belief, and soon we'll look at that more deeply. But right now, if you step back, you can't absolutely know this belief is true, can you?"

Almost everyone sees that his or her belief is not objectively true. And in this clear seeing, the tight grip of the belief loosens a little. If you can see that it's not true, you are starting to wake up from the trance of this belief.

So, answer the question: Even if you are convinced your belief is true, is it actually true?

Sub-Questions

All of these are variations on, "Is this belief true?"

> Are you absolutely certain that it's true?
>
> Even though it feels true, is it really true?
>
> Is there a chance it's not completely true?
>
> Is it always true in all situations?
>
> Couldn't the opposite be just as true?
>
> Do you have this belief or does this belief have you?

Question six starts to look at the impact this belief is having on your life.

Question 6:
Is This Belief Working For You?

The sixth question in the Unstuck Process is, "Is this belief working for you?"

By this time you're likely seeing that it isn't working at all. The belief, the feeling, the avoidance, the reactions are clearly not getting you what you want.

Heck, you just want to organize that damn closet! Organizing a closet makes you feel good about yourself. And it's relatively simple, doesn't take a long time, and costs virtually nothing (unless you spring for some fancy storage boxes).

Yes, sooner or later you'll probably get around to it. But look at the wreckage you've left in the wake of the belief that got triggered when you just thought about organizing your closet.

If you think this belief is working for you, perhaps you don't know what working is!

So, admit it, it's not working for you. It's not serving you in any useful way. It's hurting you. It's eroding your self-esteem.

Aren't you tired of it already?

One of the hallmarks of constrictive beliefs is that they don't enhance your life in any substantial way. Just the opposite. In fact, they greatly detract from your quality of life.

The beliefs about closet organizing might seem a little trivial. But the one about giving presentations obviously has more serious consequences to your business.

A change in perspective

If we asked the following question when we were struggling, resisting and avoiding, our perspective could shift quite quickly:

> *"I'm really struggling with making videos because I'll make a fool of myself. Is this belief really working for me?"*

> *"I can never seem to get around to writing that article because I'm not a good writer. Is this belief helping me?"*

> *"Nobody is interested in my services because they think they're ineffective. How well is this belief serving me?"*

Obviously none of these beliefs are working for you. So you might as well admit it. These beliefs all result in dead ends. As soon as we believe these, all forward motion stops. The goal that was so important to you fades in importance. A project you started a few weeks ago is forgotten. Any enthusiasm you had about something withers away.

I hope you're starting to see how debilitating these limiting, constrictive beliefs are. They literally suck the life out of you.

Not convinced yet?

Take a moment to think of all the great ideas, plans and projects you wanted to accomplish in your life, in your work or in your business.

Weren't you excited about these plans and projects?

But how many of them did you start, let alone complete? Instead of enjoying the results of accomplishing those things, you're left with the reasons and excuses why you didn't finish them.

Reasons or excuses might console you, but they do not equal in any way the possible results you intended to realize.

You can either feel bad about these missed opportunities or you can start to get real and admit your culpability in not following through. You can admit that you were sidelined by a constrictive, limited, fearful belief.

And you never asked yourself if this belief was really true or if it was actually working for you.

I sometimes call Question #6, the "Dr. Phil Question." After a guest on his show has confessed to all kinds of destructive behaviors and actions, Dr. Phil often asks, "How's that working for you?" In an interview with Oprah, Dr. Phil said, "When I ask that, I genuinely mean it. How is what you're doing working for you? Are you getting what you really want and need?"

It's a powerful question that puts a finishing touch on the question, "Is that true?"

"OK, you're not doing follow-up calls because you believe you'll be humiliated. Can you really know that's true? And how is believing that working for you?"

I've found the answer to these goes something like this: "Well not really; I can't know that I'll be humiliated, in fact, it's pretty unlikely. And no, that belief is not working for me; it prevents me from getting new clients I could easily be getting."

Sub-Questions

Below are other versions of, "Is this belief working for you?"

>Is this helping you get the results you want?
>
>If you keep holding onto this, where will it lead?
>
>Does this belief inspire and motivate you?
>
>Is there a stress-free way to hold onto this belief?
>
>Is there a peaceful way to hold onto this belief?
>
>What's going to happen if you keep believing this?
>
>Is this belief expansive or constrictive?
>
>How long do you want to keep arguing for this?

At this point, you might be asking, "Why do I continue to get hooked by constrictive beliefs like this? Why do they continue to hijack my goals, my intentions and dreams?"

With the next two questions in the Unstuck Process we'll explore exactly why with the "cost–payoff dynamic."

How's that working for you?

Question 7:
What Are the Costs?

The seventh question in the Unstuck Process is, "What are the costs of attaching to this belief?"

When it comes to beliefs, or avoidance for that matter, each is in a dynamic balance of cost and payoff.

We'll cover payoffs in the next chapter, but let's start by looking at the costs. That is, there is a cost to holding any belief, for taking an action or avoiding an action.

Let's take an avoided action from our original list, and look at the belief that's propping it up, and its cost.

Avoiding writing an article for my business.

The belief underneath this avoidance might be: "I'm not any good at writing." Or it could be, "I don't have any time for writing." Or perhaps it's, "Writing won't really help my business anyway." Or simply, "Writing is hard."

The costs of holding onto those beliefs should be obvious: You don't end up writing any articles, which slows down your goal of providing more information to your potential clients.

But costs usually go deeper than that. As long as you hold on to one or more of those beliefs, you'll keep avoiding writing, perhaps for a very long time. And since writing is so important as a self-employed professional, you could severely hold back the success of your business.

Then there are the emotional costs. Holding that belief undermines your confidence, self-esteem and enthusiasm about your business. I've see this happen many times. One little, seemingly harmless, belief can greatly undermine your business success.

You don't have to look very deep to identify the many costs of attaching to or identifying with a belief.

Now let's revisit an avoidance we explored earlier.

I'm avoiding planning our next vacation.

A vacation is a pleasant thing, right? So what is there to avoid? Well, how about these beliefs: "Our vacation ideas are no fun. Vacations cost too much. Our last vacation was a disaster."

If you're thinking thoughts like that, of course you'll put off planning your vacation.

So, what's the cost of those beliefs? Well, if you finally go, there's a good chance you'll end up arguing again, spending too much money and having another vacation disaster!

Are you starting to see that limiting beliefs often become self-fulfilling prophecies? You believe it and it happens. And the costs pile up. Vacations become associated with stress, not relaxation. And so you avoid going on vacation. And then, if you're in a relationship, it becomes strained.

The thing to clearly understand is that limiting beliefs have real costs. These costs are not uplifting. They drag you down, hurt your self-worth, create conflicts and result in failures.

When we're articulating a belief, we usually think it's harmless and that we're just reporting the truth. "Vacations cost too much."

That happened to be one of my deeply held beliefs for some time. My wife and I went on a vacation to Italy early in our marriage, and my penny-pinching nearly ruined the vacation for both of us. The belief was, "We're spending too much money."

When I finally became conscious of this cost (I won't embarrass myself to say how long it took), I simply stopped my penny-pinching ways. And my fears of spending too extravagantly never happened. Now on vacations, we enjoy great meals, see more sights and have more fun by spending a little extra. It hardly breaks the bank.

What are the real costs of those beliefs you attach to?

Until we see the costs, we are going to keep holding onto the belief and continue to avoid doing what works. But the belief literally forces us to turn a blind eye to the costs.

It may take a little time and effort to list all the costs of a particular belief. Here are a few costs of various beliefs, to help you "prime the pump."

- You don't get the results you want
- Your self-esteem decreases
- You under-earn in your work or business
- You have poor health or vitality
- You have little fun or recreation in your life
- You damage important relationships
- Your talents and skills are undeveloped
- You lack fulfillment
- You fail to make a contribution

Remember, these aren't just words. The costs are real. They are often painful and result in feelings of regret, guilt and loss. Nobody I've worked with was grateful for these costs; nobody was happy that they had paid them.

Now take a few minutes to write down all the costs of holding onto your belief that leads to avoidance.

Sub-Questions

Here are some other follow-up questions to, "What are the costs of attaching to this belief?"

- Exactly how high is the cost of this belief?

Is holding onto this belief worth the high cost?

Do you want to keep paying the costs of this belief?

How high would the cost have to be before you gave up this belief?

Now that you're aware of the costs of holding onto the belief, how do you feel about the belief?

In the next chapter we'll look at the payoff we get from holding on to fearful, limiting beliefs.

*The costs are high,
and the costs are real.*

Question 8:
What Is the Payoff?

The eighth question in the Unstuck Process is a double question, "What is the payoff of attaching to this belief?" and "Is that payoff real, and is it worth it?"

The first question sometimes confuses people. "Well, I certainly see the costs of holding onto this belief, but I don't see a payoff. I really don't get anything out of holding onto it."

Let's look more closely at the cost–payoff dynamic.

Everything you do in life, every thought and belief you have, without exception, comes with a cost and a payoff. Let's look at an action you're familiar with.

Let's say you've developed the practice of exercising regularly.

The cost of exercising regularly is effort, time and some soreness in your body. The payoff is good health, more strength, endurance, flexibility and energy.

If you perceive that the payoff of exercising is greater than the cost, you'll keep exercising. If you perceive the cost exceeds the payoff, you'll stop exercising.

There is no exception to this! Whatever is greater, the payoff or the cost, determines the actions you'll take.

Now let's take another practice – smoking. This also has a cost and a payoff.

The cost of smoking is poor heath, including several diseases, such as emphysema, lung cancer and heart disease.

Those costs are pretty high, aren't they? And because many people take these costs seriously, they don't start smoking, or they ultimately stop.

The payoff to smoking is the immediate release you feel when your smoking addiction is satisfied. Plus, you get to look cool!

That momentary satisfaction you get from smoking seems like a small payoff in comparison to the cost, but if you keep smoking, that payoff has won out, hasn't it? The relief you get from a fix is a tremendously strong force.

Let's take another example from our avoidance list in Chapter 1 and look at the payoffs you get from that avoidance.

I'm avoiding going to the dentist.

The belief that supports this avoidance might be something like: "Going to the dentist is painful."

And the costs of not going to the dentist are pretty obvious: gum disease, cavities, toothaches, expensive crowns. You may avoid the dentist now, but sooner or later you'll go, and the cost will usually be higher than if you went more often.

So what's the payoff of not going to the dentist?

I've observed that the most common payoff for just about any avoidance is the same: We get to stay in our comfort zones.

It's important to realize how much this drives avoidance.

When we avoid, we perceive a real and immediate payoff that makes us forget the cost. When we avoid, we get to survive by being more comfortable and less uncomfortable.

And what's another word for uncomfortable? Pain.

Yes, much of our avoidance is driven by the avoidance of imagined pain. We are literally addicted to avoiding pain. Just like smoking. Smoking relieves the pain that comes when we don't smoke for a while. So we keep smoking.

Some people get lung cancer and continue to smoke.

It's a little easier to see this when we are physically addicted to something such as nicotine, drugs or alcohol. The payoff is more obvious.

Imagined pain can have just as strong a pull. If we think taking action will result in pain of any kind, we avoid it without thinking. It's an automatic reaction. This reaction operates in the background, subverting and undermining our best intentions.

I've seen this in operation with hundreds of clients. One of the biggest areas of avoidance, for self-employed people, is making follow-up calls. This occurs when you call someone you met (who might be a potential client), to talk about your business and to explore working with them.

People avoid follow-up like the plague.

Why? Because they get to avoid possible rejection from the prospective client. It might not go well; the person might not be interested; they might feel you're being pushy. So, it's easier to avoid the call. The payoff of staying comfortable and avoiding discomfort is accomplished!

Rejection is one of the most intense pains a person can experience. We arrange our lives to be accepted and not rejected. We think of rejection as embarrassing, devastating, humiliating, and mortifying. It's not what we want to experience in any way, shape, or form.

The payoff is winning by losing. As perverse as that may seem, almost everyone does this in certain areas of their lives. With this understanding, the cause of avoidance comes clearly into focus.

Any situation, action, task, project, discipline, undertaking, practice, chore or job that triggers associations of discomfort or pain of any kind, are avoided at all costs.

As we've already observed, the costs can be very high. But avoiding the imagined pain becomes the higher priority.

Now, in many cases, avoiding pain makes perfect sense.

Because I don't want to hurt myself or die, I don't jump off high cliffs, run in traffic, juggle chainsaws or tell my wife she should lose a few pounds.

Doing those things would be stupid and a true (not imagined) threat to my survival.

But not making follow-up calls because you might be rejected? Yes, the association is painful, but is that rejection really going to happen and be as painful as you imagine?

This is the crux of the matter.

The second payoff question is: Is that payoff real, and is it worth it?

Your payoff of staying comfortable and avoiding pain is often completely imaginary. That is, the pain will simply not happen. When you make a follow-up call, they will not send a hit man to take you out, let alone reject and humiliate you.

About the worst that can happen is that they won't be interested right now. How terrible is that? You could survive that, couldn't you?

> When you go to the dentist it won't be as painful as you think it will be. Novocaine actually works!
>
> Planning your vacation usually won't end in disaster.
>
> Cleaning out your closet won't really be a nightmare.

The problem is, we don't think rationally about these things. We are triggered because of past associations, usually by something that happened to us a long time ago.

Let's look at a typical avoidance scenario.

You think of asking for a raise. Just the thought of asking for a raise triggers a belief based on the avoidance of pain:

"They'll just say no, anyway." You feel bad, fearful, weak. You put off asking for a raise until next month. End of scenario.

You think you've dodged a bullet, and you feel some relief, but you still don't feel very good. After all, you usually don't get a raise unless you ask for it. But that fear-based belief won out again. And you'll pay a cost for holding onto that belief for some time to come.

However, when we apply the "Unstuck Process" to this belief, we undermine the belief and things start to look very different.

You think of asking for a raise and your fear-based belief is triggered. This time, you pull out an "Unstuck Worksheet" and put your thoughts on paper.

What am I avoiding? I'm avoiding asking for a raise.

How does that feel? It feels scary asking for the raise because I might not get it and would feel even worse.

How do I react when I believe I'll be rejected when I ask for the raise? I just avoid asking; I make excuses; I think it will be better to ask later; I don't stand up for myself; I feel resentful and like a wimp.

What is the belief under avoiding asking for a raise? I'd have to believe I'd be rejected.

Is this belief true? Well, I can't really know for sure. I've asked for raises before and gotten them.

Is this belief working for me? Obviously not!

What is the cost of attaching to this belief? Well, I don't get the raise, I lose some of my self-esteem, reinforce this avoidance in the future, and I lose the respect of others.

What is the payoff of attaching to this belief? I get to stay in my comfort zone; I avoid being rejected and feeling bad.

Is this payoff real, and is it worth it? Probably not. The cost is much more real. I can make a good argument for getting a raise, and if I don't get it, I don't need to take it personally. It's really not going to be as painful as I think it is. What's the worst that could happen? My boss could say no. Perhaps he'd say yes.

Once you've gone though this whole process you may see your situation completely differently. You have seen through your automatic reactions and your fear. You've seen the real costs of avoidance and the unreal payoff of staying comfortable and avoiding pain.

At this point, you might start to notice that you feel a little differently. You may start to feel hopeful, courageous, creative and bold.

Let me give you a final metaphor for how beliefs limit us.

Imagine that there's a haunted house in your neighborhood. It's really old and scary. And there's a legend that the previous owner hid a lot of money and jewels in the house that were never found.

But there's also a legend that the house is haunted by a murderous ghost, who is protecting the treasure. And because of this, nobody has had the courage to go into the house and search for the money and jewels.

There is an obvious cost for not going into the house and searching for the treasure – you won't find the treasure and get rich. The payoff for not going into the house is that you'll stay safe and the ghost won't murder you.

But what if you discovered that the ghost wasn't real? It was a hoax that was made up by some people who wanted the treasure for themselves. With this new information, your previous fear turns into excitement.

When you discover that the ghost story is a hoax, everything is different. The "staying-safe-payoff" is no longer valid. You know you won't come to any harm if you search the house. So you explore the house and actually end up finding some money and jewels.

The Unstuck Process opens up new possibilities by systematically undermining your limiting beliefs. The process never asks you to feel differently or behave differently, but to be honest with yourself and to tell the truth.

As they say, the truth will set you free. However, it might tick you off a little at first to notice how you've set yourself up for failure by avoiding something that you really wanted, for a payoff that doesn't really exist.

Faced with this reality, it's hard for the belief to keep arguing for its point of view. It just may start to drop away without any effort on your part.

Before you move on, write down the answers to the two questions about payoffs and be very clear whether or not the apparent payoff is real or not.

Sub-Questions

In addition to these two questions about the payoff of attaching to the belief, you might ask some of these follow-up questions.

> What do you really get out of this belief that's so important?
>
> What discomfort or pain are you avoiding?
>
> Is the possible discomfort of taking action all that bad?
>
> Is this payoff more important than the costs?
>
> Is this payoff really fulfilling and satisfying?
>
> Isn't the possible pain largely imaginary?
>
> What's more important, comfort or results?
>
> What's the worst thing that could happen if you stopped your avoidance?
>
> Would you rather be right than get what you want?

In the final four questions of the process we'll explore what lies beyond these limiting beliefs.

The payoff, once again, was simply not there.

Question 9:
Who Would You Be Without this Belief?

The ninth question in the Unstuck Process is, "Who would you be if it were impossible to attach to this belief?"

If I'm facilitating the Unstuck Process, I'll often ask another, supporting question: "What if you woke up tomorrow morning with the same circumstances, but the belief never arose once during the day. Who would you be then?"

All the questions in the process, up to this point, have been focused on your actions, feelings, and beliefs, and how they impact you. This question and the following three questions are quite different.

This question asks you to imagine who you would be without that belief. Sometimes this is a little hard to grasp. The belief seems so real, so ever-present. How could the belief not be there?

You're being asked to exercise your imagination.

When people jump into this, these are the kind of answers I hear: "I'd feel free, unencumbered. I would feel more energetic and excited. I'd feel as if a burden had been lifted from my shoulders. I would feel there was hope and a way to finally make this work. I wouldn't be struggling or stuck anymore."

Sometimes I use this metaphor: Imagine you are walking around in life with a one hundred pound bag of cement on your shoulders. For a long time you never really noticed it, but it prevented you from doing many things. You were also stooped over and in pain.

Then one day somebody pointed out that you were carrying this heavy burden. You denied it at first; after all, it had become a habit. But then you took a closer look and saw how much it cost you to carry it around. Wouldn't you just drop it without any struggle or effort?

That bag of cement is your limiting, fearful belief. Without it, everything changes, doesn't it?

What if I told you that you were carrying around not one, but many bags of cement? Imagine what it would be like if you became aware of all of them, and ultimately let them go. What would that be like?

As you continue to work through the Unstuck Process you'll discover many of these heavy burdens you've been shouldering for years. No wonder some parts of your life are such a struggle. No wonder you avoid so many things!

The act of unburdening yourself from a limiting belief can be very freeing, very liberating. You just might take on the project of discovering every limiting belief you can find, and subjecting it to the questions in this process.

I've discovered an important side-benefit to this process. Once you explore a belief like this, many other similar beliefs drop as well, as they were so closely connected.

I've worked with clients who did this process just once or twice, and they found they were no longer avoiding a certain activity. They also noticed they were avoiding less in other areas of their lives. The process seemed to create a momentum that helped them naturally unburden themselves.

If you haven't done so yet, write down the answer to the question, "Who would you be if it were impossible to attach to this belief?"

Sub-Questions

In addition to the question, "who you would be if it were impossible to attach to this belief," you might also ask:

> How good would you be willing for it to be?
>
> Would that lift a great burden off you shoulders if you no longer had this belief?
>
> Can you imagine a life without this belief?
>
> Would it be OK with you if this belief dissolved?

Question 10 will take us one step further.

For how long will you shoulder that burden?

Not everything is possible.
But anything is possible.
What's possible for you?

Question 10:
What Possibilities Might Open Up for You?

The tenth question in the Unstuck Process is, "What possibilities might open up to you if you no longer identified with this belief?"

Without being burdened by the old belief, you might start feeling more energetic, enthusiastic and creative. Stretch your imagination a little further. What would you do with that energy, enthusiasm and creativity?

What possibilities might open up for you now that the limiting belief is no longer in the way?

When you get to this point in the process you may find yourself thinking quite differently. That belief was like a suppression button. Once released, the possibilities may seem unlimited.

> What would you take on at work or in your business?
>
> What projects would you finally start (or complete)?
>
> What people would you re-connect with?
>
> Where would you go on vacation?
>
> What would you read or study?
>
> What would you do for you health?

Doing the Unstuck Process just once may not open up new possibilities in every area of your life. But if you keep doing it regularly, you may discover a whole new world of possibilities in areas you hadn't even considered before.

There are no right answers here. There are no specific goals you should have. The opening of possibilities is a natural, human impulse. Who you are, beyond your limiting beliefs, is magnificent and capable.

As you continue to do this process, new and exciting areas of your life will open up to you without struggle or effort. They will be a natural expression of who you are.

Now, take a few minutes to write down as many of those new possibilities as you can.

Sub-Questions

Use these questions to stimulate new possibilities without the limiting belief:

> What projects would you do without this belief?
>
> How would your energy change without this belief?
>
> What other avoidances might drop without this belief?
>
> Where would you be in a year without this belief?
>
> Where would you be in five years without this belief?
>
> If you could live without this belief, what other beliefs could you live without?
>
> How would living without this belief change your work life, your business, your love life, your community, the world?

Question 11 is about your willingness to just be who you are.

Question 11:
Is it OK to Just Be Who You Are?

The eleventh question in the Unstuck Process is, "Is it OK just to be who you are without having this belief anymore?"

The answer to this will be a very clear yes or no. My experience has been that the answer is almost always yes.

You've just looked at who you would be without this belief and what possibilities might open up for you without this belief, so it's a natural final step to just be who you are without this belief.

I've found that it's useful to confirm this.

For a very long time, it hasn't been OK for you to be without this belief. It's been a matter of survival to hold onto it for dear life. This belief has been one of your touchstones to reality. It's not that you've *had* this belief, but that you've *been* this belief.

Without this belief, who are you?

The mind is always seeking to identify with something. We literally become our beliefs, our feelings, our bodies, our actions, and our identity in the world.

But as your beliefs let go of their grip, aren't you still you? Is there any single thought or feeling you have that's really you? Every thought or feeling simply arises in your awareness and then fades from awareness.

Some thoughts and feelings are a little more persistent. They stick around longer and we become attached to them. But with this process you'll discover that no thought, belief or feeling is permanent. Beliefs come and go.

The only permanent thing (and it's not really a thing) is a presence, which is aware of your thoughts, feelings and beliefs. That never goes away. It's always aware. It's always present.

So you might say that who you are is awareness or an aware presence.

Awareness is the only constant.

Awareness is something you can count on and rest in. It has no agendas or limitations or points of view or beliefs or constraints. It just is.

It's awareness that answered the questions. It's awareness that remains after the questions have been answered. It's awareness that gives birth to possibilities.

So, be clear: Are you OK with being just who you are, that is, an aware presence, without this belief (or any fearful beliefs)?

Sub-Questions

We've been attached to certain beliefs for so long, it can be hard to imagine living without them. Here are some other questions to help imagine that possibility.

> Would it be OK if the belief just dropped away?
>
> How are you different without this belief?
>
> Are you happier without this belief?
>
> Are you less stressed without this belief?
>
> Are you more peaceful without this belief?
>
> Are you more you without this belief?
>
> Are you more alive without this belief?
>
> Isn't it great being you without this belief?

Finally, the only thing left is to choose what to do next.

Question 12:
What Will You Do Next?

The twelfth and final question in the Unstuck Process is, "What will you do next?"

Since you've declared that you could, in fact, be OK just as you are, without the belief, you are free to explore new possibilities without the belief.

Who you are is possibility. You are an open space in which creation, appreciation, engagement and productivity all naturally appear. It's not hard work. It's natural. It is not a struggle. It just flows.

But up to this point, your firmly held beliefs have clouded over this effortless being. Things have looked difficult, stressful, unpleasant or annoying.

But you've unraveled the trance of the belief. You see its cost and its payoff and its unreality. A firmly held belief that controlled your actions is no longer in charge.

At this point you may feel a lot lighter, freer, and happier for no apparent reason.

What are you going to do now?

How does the thing you were avoiding look now? Does it look easier, more interesting, more inviting? Can you see yourself taking this on like a game to be played instead of a burden to be shouldered? Do you see how doing this thing might be fun, exciting and rewarding?

Now, if you've read this far but you haven't actually done the process, I urge you to print out an Unstuck Worksheet and, using the book as a guide, go through all the questions step-by-step.

Pick something that you've been struggling with or avoiding for some time. Pick something where you really feel stuck and at a loss about what to do. Pick something where you feel hopeless.

But don't do this process to get better. You already *are* better. The light is already on. It's just that it's veiled by the belief so completely that you can't see it. Uncover the belief one step at a time and the light will ultimately shine through.

When that happens you'll know what to do and find it easy to learn how to do it.

Let the good times roll!

Sub-Questions

What will you do next is a pretty wide open question. You could also ask more specific questions:

> What incomplete project will you get done?
>
> What's something you'll get organized?
>
> What will you do next at work?
>
> What will you do next in your business?
>
> What will you do to relax?
>
> What will you do for your body?
>
> What will you do next in your relationships?
>
> Where will your next vacation be?
>
> What's something new you'll learn about?
>
> What fun thing will you do next?
>
> What challenging thing will you do next?

About You

The Unstuck Process is simple to do

But it's not always easy

These questions don't seem that deep

But they will penetrate you, startle you

Awaken you to something new but familiar

Without attachments to your beliefs

What do you have?

You have freedom, spaciousness

You have You

What more could you want?

All the best,

Robert Middleton

Take Action

To take action to do this process is a paradox. I'm asking you to take action before you've figured out how to get past stuckness and avoidance. Many people may read this book from beginning to end but then never do the process. I hope you're not one of them. It would be a little like reading all about swimming but never jumping into the pool!

A few ideas might help.

You can't do this process wrong. Just start with the first question and then the second and then third until you're done. Like everything else, you'll get better at it the more you do it.

Use the worksheet. The worksheet makes this process super easy to do. It has all the questions of the process; you just need to fill in the answers. You are free to duplicate it and use it whenever you want.

www.actionplan.com/up/Unstuck_Process.doc

Don't do the process with the focus on changing yourself.

It isn't about changing, but about letting go. What you'll find beyond your avoidance is a perfectly capable person whose possibilities are virtually unlimited.

Do the process to get at the truth. Do it like a private investigator who is objectively collecting the facts, one at a time. By the end of the process, the answer will emerge.

Acknowledgements

Many people have greatly influenced how I developed and fine-tuned this process.

Byron Katie – Without Katie, there wouldn't be an Unstuck Process. Her approach to inquiry is at the heart of this process.

www.thework.com

Rupert Spira – Rupert is a powerful, kind and wise teacher of non-duality. Rupert helped me finally understand who I really am underneath all my beliefs and limitations.

www.non-duality.rupertspira.com

Arjuna Ardagh – Arjuna is another amazing teacher whose work inspired the creation of this process. He opened up a new world of working with clients to create breakthroughs.

www.awakeningcoachingtraining.com

My Clients – I have tested and fine tuned variations of this process over several years with my clients. It is their results and breakthroughs that have inspired me to make this available to more people.

All the Questions & Sub-Questions

This is a quick guide through all the 12 questions and sub-questions that you can refer to as you fill out the worksheet. If you are facilitating this process for someone else, you can also use this as a guide.

1. Where are you stuck or what are you avoiding?

> What is something you're resisting?
>
> What is something you're doing that you don't want to be doing?
>
> What is an attitude you have that's not working for you?
>
> What are your judgments about another person?

2. What is your primary feeling when you experience this?

> What sensations are you experiencing in your body?

3. How do you behave when you experience this?

> Describe your avoidance behavior in detail.
>
> What else are you avoiding when you avoid that?
>
> Is there an attitude or mindset associated with the avoidance?
>
> Is this behavior habitual and automatic?
>
> What are you thinking or saying to yourself when you're avoiding?
>
> Does your mood change when you're avoiding?

4. What is the belief underneath the avoidance?

> What am I telling myself when I'm avoiding that thing?
>
> What is a phrase I keep repeating inside my head?
>
> Can I find the belief underneath my feeling?
>
> What would I have to believe to continue avoiding that?
>
> What am I afraid would happen to me if I stopped avoiding and took action?

5. You're convinced the belief is true, but is it?

> Are you absolutely certain that it's true?
>
> Even though it feels true, is it really true?
>
> Is there a chance it's not completely true?
>
> Is it always true in all situations?
>
> Couldn't the opposite be just as true?
>
> Do you have this belief or does this belief have you?

6. Is this belief working for you?

> Is this helping you get the results you want?
>
> If you keep holding onto that, where will it lead?
>
> Does this belief inspire and motivate you?
>
> Is there a stress-free way to hold onto this belief?
>
> Is there a peaceful way to hold onto this belief?
>
> What's going to happen if you keep believing this?
>
> Is this belief expansive or constrictive?
>
> How long do you want to keep arguing for that?

7. What are the costs of attaching to this belief?

Exactly how high is the cost of this belief?

Is holding onto this belief worth the high cost?

Do you want to keep paying the costs of this belief?

How high would the costs have to be before you gave up this belief?

Now that you're aware of the costs of holding onto the belief, how do you feel about the belief?

8. a) What is the payoff of attaching to this belief?
b) Is the payoff real and is it worth it?

What do you really get out of this belief that's so important?

What discomfort or pain are you avoiding?

Is the possible discomfort of taking action all that bad?

Is the payoff more important than the costs?

Is the payoff really fulfilling and satisfying?

Isn't the possible pain largely imaginary?

What's more important, comfort or results?

What's the worst thing that could happen if you stopped your avoidance?

Would you rather be right than get what you want?

9. Who would you be and how would things be if it were impossible to attach to this belief?

How good would you be willing for it to be?

Would that lift a great burden off you shoulders if you no longer had this belief?

Can you imagine a life without this belief?

Would it be OK with you if this belief dissolved?

10. What possibilities might open up to you if you no longer identified with this belief?

> What projects would you do without this belief?
>
> How would your energy change without this belief?
>
> What other avoidances might drop without this belief?
>
> Where would you be in a year without this belief?
>
> Where would you be in five years without this belief?
>
> If you could live without this belief, what other beliefs could you live without?
>
> How would living without this belief change your work life, your business, your love life, your community, the world?

11. It is OK just to be who you are without having this belief anymore?

> Would it be OK if the belief just dropped away?
>
> How are you different without this belief?
>
> Are you happier without this belief?
>
> Are you less stressed without this belief?
>
> Are you more peaceful without this belief?
>
> Are you more you without this belief?
>
> Are you more alive without this belief?
>
> Isn't it great being you without this belief?

12. What will you do next?

> What incomplete project will you get done?
>
> What's something you'll get organized?
>
> What will you do next at work?
>
> What will you do next in your business?

What will you do to relax?

What will you do for your body?

What will you do next in your relationships?

Where will your next vacation be?

What's something new you'll learn about?

What fun thing will you do next?

What challenging thing will you do next?

About Robert Middleton

Robert has been working with Independent Professionals as a marketing coach and consultant since 1984. He has worked with thousands of people to get past their limiting beliefs about what is possible in their businesses, marketing, and in their lives.

Robert offers courses and workshops on the Unstuck Process. Just visit his website for details:

www.theunstuckprocess.com

Want Some Support?

It can be useful to get facilitation for the Unstuck Process. If you are stuck in a limiting belief that won't seem to let go and you are stuck in avoidance, I'd be happy to work with you. I offer an affordable 3-session package where we'll identify your beliefs and help you work through them completely.

I also offer an 8-session Course on the Unstuck Process. This course is especially helpful if you want to facilitate the process with others and go deeper with the process yourself.

Sessions: www.theunstuckprocess.com/sessions

Courses: www.theunstuckprocess/courses

Printed in Great Britain
by Amazon